故園畫憶

庚寅中秋

韩启德题

韓啓德

故园画忆系列

Memory of the Old Home in Sketches

龚滩古镇

Gongtan Ancient Town

周鼎　绘画 撰文

Sketches & Notes by Zhou Ding

學苑出版社

Academy Press

图书在版编目（CIP）数据

龚滩古镇 / 周鼎绘画、撰文. — 北京：学苑出版社，2015.6

（故园画忆系列）

ISBN 978-7-5077-4783-6

Ⅰ. ①龚… Ⅱ. ①周… Ⅲ. ①乡镇—概况—重庆市—图集

Ⅳ. ①K927.195-64

中国版本图书馆CIP数据核字（2015）第118741号

出 版 人：孟　白
责任编辑：洪文雄
出版发行：学苑出版社
社　　址：北京市丰台区南方庄2号院1号楼
邮政编码：100079
网　　址：www.book001.com
电子信箱：xueyuanpress@163.com
销售电话：010-67601001（销售部）、67603091（总编室）
经　　销：全国新华书店
印 刷 厂：北京信彩瑞禾印刷厂
开本尺寸：889×1194 1/24
印　　张：7.5
字　　数：160千字
图　　幅：80幅
版　　次：2015年6月北京第1版
印　　次：2015年6月北京第1次印刷
定　　价：56.00元

目 录

Contents

崖上古镇　涅槃重生（代序）

千里乌江，千年流淌，成就千年古镇；

百里画廊，百座吊楼，再现土家风光。

位于乌江边的龚滩古镇位列巴渝名镇之首，实为巴人遗风之瑰宝、土家精神之代表。民风淳朴，历史悠远，吊楼倚江、石径蜿蜒，百代相传、安土乐业，延续着3000年巴人血脉。龚滩古镇已有1700年的历史，在明朝万历之年，龚滩所依乌江岸边的凤凰山发生巨石滑坡，阻断了乌江，形成了险滩，正如《酉阳县志》所记载“大江之中，横列巨石，大者如宅，小者如牛，激水雷鸣、惊涛雪喷”，此时，乌江大船已无法航行，只有小船可勉强通过。无论上水下水，载货船只到此必经起卸重装，卸载货物均需在此周转，依靠人力上下搬运。但乌江的断航给龚滩人创造了一条发展的新路，也吸引来了各地商贾云集龚滩，使它迅速成为川黔湘鄂交接的武陵山区的物流中心，各种货场的集散中心，乌江航运的发展使龚滩逐渐走向繁荣，商贾云集，通江达海，成就了龚滩的繁华。

1949年后，在现代交通发展到这里之前，乌江航运还是武陵山区与外界沟通的唯一通道，龚滩依然是酉阳秀山地区进入重庆成都的重要驿站。随着公路、铁路的开通，陆上交通取代了水运，龚滩作为交通、商贸、物流的中心地位被完全取代，昔日繁华的龚滩逐渐沉寂下来，封闭起来。

新世纪乌江阶梯电站的开发惊醒了寂静的龚滩，其中彭水电站坝前蓄水达到294米线时，要将龚滩古镇全部淹没于水下。在此之前，曾做过两次古镇的迁建方案。该镇虽在2000年被命名为重庆市历史文化名镇，但当时都认为该镇将被拆除的命运是不可阻挡的，因此，尽管龚滩被列入巴渝古镇之首，重庆市也没有再将其申报国家历史文化名镇，而保存状况不如龚滩的龙潭镇和石柱县西沱镇均在2003年建设部公布的第一批历史文化名镇名单时榜上有名，眼看着1700年的历史龚滩古镇终将沉入江底，各界人士无不痛心疾首。

古镇即将被淹没的消息，不仅为广大人民群众不舍，有志之士也给予奔走呼吁，但终因该镇即非国家级及省级历史文化名镇名村，也非国家级省级文物保护单位，全镇列入县保的古建筑民居也仅存八处。开发商对八处被列入县级文保单位的建筑，将依据《文物保护法》的要求，参考三峡文物保护的作法，予以异地迁建保护，其他建于不同时代、不同形式的吊脚楼均就地拆除，按一般民房予以赔偿安置。为保住龚滩古镇，当地政府反复与开发商交涉，为此由重庆市移民局主持、重庆市文化局参与，再一次组织由文物、建设方和当地政府参加的专家组对龚滩古镇进行一次全面考察并提出处理意见。我有幸参加了这一次现场考察，并担任了此次考察的专家组长。2005 年 10 月 14 至 15 日，我和专家组的同志们用两天时间，沿着龚滩古镇分上中下三条线。在绵延 1.6 千米的沿江路上往返多次，对每一栋吊脚楼深入调查，与屋主人攀谈。无论是在古镇的石板小径上，还是在乌江边，看着全镇极富立体感的吊脚楼的立面，给我留下了深深的印象。我暗自思量，龚滩古镇正处于乌江百里画廊的核心区，亿万年生成的自然风光与千百年沿袭的风土民情，都是中华民族珍贵的遗产，一定要设法将古镇完整保护下来。现场考察结束后，专家组进行讨论，我提出整体保护古镇的想法，经过反复沟通。大家终于达成一致意见，同时我们也提出有部分后来改建、新建的与古镇风貌不协调的建筑以及有些在原吊脚楼旁加建的部分与古镇风貌完全不同的建筑不能作为古镇风貌保留。最终以专家组名义向政府提交了一个考察纪要，基本确定了整体保护古镇风貌的格调。

又经过一年的时间，各方终于达成共识，古镇的迁建保护工程开始了。我出任了该工程的总监理工程师。当时我就下定决心，要让世人看到一个保持了原来风貌的新龚滩，不仅建筑风貌不改变，而且千百年来当地居民几百年形成的生产、生活方式、传统习俗都要原汁原味保留。彭水电站的建设不是龚滩古镇生命的终结，而是一个古镇的新生的庆贺。为了真实记录下古镇的原始风貌，我特地请了周鼎先生到古镇来体验，希望他用画笔真实的记录下古镇的原貌，以便于搬迁后的新龚滩做一对比。

周鼎先生自幼喜爱美术，自初中就读于专门的美术中学——郑州铁六中，中学毕业后考入中央民族大学，师从高润喜学习，毕业后又赴俄罗斯深造，在著名的列宾美术学院读预科，后就读于圣彼得堡国立师范美术学院，师从俄罗斯功勋艺术家库兹米乔夫，具有扎实的基本功和良好的欣赏能力。当我向周鼎提出用钢笔画来画龚滩的古建筑时，这对他无疑是一个挑战。他原来主修油画，而钢笔画是一个需要耐得寂寞的慢活，对于一个年轻人来说，也相当于是锤炼自己性子的一个机会。他到了龚滩，看到这里高耸的吊脚楼、蜿蜒的石板路、古老的黄葛树、小巧的天井院、奔腾的乌江、壁立的江岸……无不带来心灵的震撼。他承诺用自己的画笔记录下古镇的一切。自2007年之初在龚滩古镇考察后，就全身心投入到绘画工作中。几年来他把自己的业余时间大部分投入到了龚滩古镇的画作中。仅一幅古镇的全图，就有近四米长。据他讲历时六个月，仅针管笔就用了一百余支，由此可想整个古镇全部画完是多么大的一个工作量啊，而这一切都是在没有任何报酬情况下完成的，除了一份对古镇的热爱和对事业的执着，还能有什么呢。

龚滩古镇迁建工作于三年前就搬完了，今天正以古镇的原貌展现在世人面前，古镇涅槃重生了。作为“故图画忆系列丛书”其中之一的《龚滩古镇》也即将由学苑出版社要公开出版了，看到这样的一个结果，也了结了我的一个心愿，可喜可贺。

愿古镇永存。

牛宁

2013年7月30日

An ancient town on the cliff, a phoenix rising from the ashes
(In lieu of a preface)

Wujiang River, thousands of miles long, thousands of years flowing, forming an ancient town with thousands of years of history.

Hundreds of galleries, hundreds of stilt houses, representing the glory of the Tujia people.

Gongtan Ancient Town, located by the Wujing River, has a history of 1,700 years. In the reign of Ming Emperor Wanli (1573-1620), a giant rockslide occurred on Phoenix Mountain by the Wujiang River, thus the Wujiang River was partially blocked and rapids formed. Large ships could not navigate through the watercourse; small ones could scarcely squeeze through. Whether up-stream or down-stream, cargo had to be manually off and on loaded. The suspension of shipping on the Wujiang River forced merchants to locate at Gongtan by Phoenix Mountain, bringing the town great prosperity. Transport on the Wujiang River was the sole channel of communication between Wuling mountain areas and the outside world, and Gongtan town was the crucial post house connecting Chongqing and Chengdu in the Youyang and Xiushan mountain areas.

With the development of modern transportation after 1949, Gongtan, as the center of transportation, commerce and logistics, was gradually replaced. Its former prosperity gradually faded and ceased. But the construction of a hydropower station in the new century has awaken silent Gongtan. The water storage level of Pengshui hydropower station has reached to 294 meters and the ancient Gongtan will be submerged.

This news for people reluctant to part, has caused pain for all walks of life and caused hopeful people to appeal the decision. In October 2005, an expert panel and I conducted a thorough investigation talking with the owner of each stilt house in Gongtan, tracking along the upper, middle and lower routes, walking to and fro repeatedly along the riverside stretching 1.6 kilometers. Walking on the stone path of the town or overlooking the three-dimensional stilt houses by the Wujiang River, we were deeply impressed. Gongtan is the core region of the hundred-mile Wujiang Gallery, representing billion years of natural beauty and inheriting thousand years of ethnic customs. It is one of our precious national heritages and therefore must be preserved intact by all means. After the field investigation, on behalf of all experts, we submitted to the government our summary for overall protection of Gongtan.

A year after the relocation and protection project of the town was launched, I was appointed chief supervising engineer. I was determined to show the people the new Gongtan its original charm, unchanged architectural features, pristine and unique production activities, life styles and traditional customs, which have been followed for thousands of years by the local residents.The building of the Pengshui hydropower station is not the termination of the life of Gongtan, but a celebration of its rebirth.

Mr. Zhou Ding was fond of art from his childhood, and further pursued art study in Rapin Art College and Saint Petersburg

State Normal Art College in Russia after his graduation from Minzu University of China. He has solid essential art skills and excellent abilities. My suggestion of sketching Gongtan ancient buildings in pen and ink is no doubt a big challenge to him. Oil painting was his specialty, while pen-and-ink was a labor requiring patience in loneliness. This challenge offered an opportunity for this young man to practice. When viewing the towering stilt houses, the winding stone allies, the old ficus virens, the exquisite courtyards, the rolling Wujiang River, the sheer cliffs, he was deeply thrilled. After the investigation in early 2007, he devoted himself to the sketching work. For several years, he spent most of his leisure time sketching the town. It took him 6 months and over 100 pens to finish the 4-meter-long full graphic record of the town. What a huge work it would be if every site in the town had been included. Mr. Zhou Ding, however, accomplished this task without a penny of pay. This proves his affection for the town and his passion for his artistic career.

Today's Gongtan presents its original view. It is like a phoenix rising from the ashes. This book, entitled *Gongtan Ancient Town*, as one of the *Memory of the Old Home in Sketches* will be published by Academy Press. My dream will come true when the book is released. Congratulations are certainly due!

On to eternity for Gongtan Ancient Town.

Niu Ning
July 30th, 2013

前 言

龚滩古镇坐落在重庆市酉阳土家族苗族自治县境内，位于乌江与阿蓬江交汇处的乌江东岸，因整个镇子依山崖而建，素有“崖上古镇”之称，为巴渝名镇之首。

龚滩古镇历史悠久，先秦时期，巴人就在此居住生活。据资料显示，今龚滩即古涪陵郡汉复县。唐武德二年（619 年）在黔州设洪杜县，在麟德二年（665 年）移置龚湍，即今龚滩。宋绍熙三年（1192 年）设晋潭巡检司，辖龚滩。清乾隆元年（1736 年）酉阳改直隶州，以龚滩属关隘要地，距州城遥远，治理难周，故设巡检司于此，以“统摄之”。清末民初，龚滩设分县（龚滩县佐）。

古镇地理位置十分重要，千百年来这里是入川水路的必经之路。明万历元年（1573 年）凤凰山崩塌，巨石塞江，船只不能通行，便在龚滩自然形成上下两座码头，出入巴蜀的大量货物囤积于江边，必须以人力搬运过滩，这使龚滩初具规模。清朝时各地商帮巨贾纷纷云集龚滩，此时龚滩已成为乌江流域重要的中转口岸，上运大宗食盐及日用百货，下行大量生漆、桐油、粮食，同时古镇中建起了很多客栈、商号、大屋、祠堂、会馆、庙宇，古镇繁荣可谓盛极一时。

龚滩悠久的历史、独特的地理位置，造就了古镇独具特色的自然、历史、人文景观。乌江与阿蓬江湍湍奔流；两岸悬崖峭壁鬼斧神工；古镇中以织女楼、盘龙楼为代表吊脚楼鳞次栉比；青石板铺成的老街蜿蜒曲折；川主庙、冉家祠堂等宗祠庙堂古朴雄浑；再加上古码头、古纤道、古山道、古桥、古树、古井、古碑的点缀，形成了一个美丽的画卷。

1959 年由于乌江航运的彻底整治，塞江巨石被炸，船只上下通行无阻，航行时间大大减少，龚滩失去了作为川、湘、黔物资中转和集散地的作用，古镇从此衰败。21 世纪初，彭水电站的建设再次使古镇成为人们的焦点，因修建大坝古镇不可避免的被淹没在水中，庆幸地是在文物部门努力下古镇得到了全面的保护，于 2007 年开始整体搬迁。

2007 年初应河南省古代建筑保护研究所牛宁所长邀请赴古镇考察，在惊叹跌宕起伏的古镇命运、庆幸如此完美的古镇结局的同时，被这里古朴、别致的景色深深打动，也便有了画古镇的初衷。在古镇的日子里大量写生、采集素材，之后便开始了艰难地创作过程。钢笔画与别的画种不同它技法虽然简单，用简单的技法画出丰富的效果却绝非易事，它耗费的心力却远远大于同等尺幅的油画，这批画一画便是三年，八十余张，其中那张《龚滩古镇》宽一米有余，长近四米。至此，古镇也早已搬迁完毕。

谨以此书表达对古镇的敬意和纪念。

Prologue

Gongtan Ancient Town, in Tujia-Miao Autonomous County of Youyang, in southwest China's Chongqing Municipality, is located on the east bank where the Wujiang meets the Apeng River. The entire town is built along the hillside, and therefore is named "An Ancient Town on the Cliff", ranking as the first of the famous towns in Chongqing Municipality.

Gongtan has a long history and a unique location - turbulent roiling at the confluence of the Wujiang and Apeng Rivers, cliffs on both sides displaying the great works of nature, stilt houses like Zhinü and Panlong close rows, old green, winding slate alleys, temples and halls, such as Chuanzhu Temple and Ran Family Ancestral Hall, shining with power and pristine beauty, and with the embellishment of old docks, old track roads, old mountain paths, old bridges, old trees, old wells, and old stone monuments - a glorious vision of the ancient town is eventually constructed.

In 2007, I was invited to do an analysis of the town. After sketching and collecting lots of material, I began my journey of creation. Pen drawing is different from any other painting. It is no easy job to draw simple sketches exhibiting rich effects. All the effort I paid greatly exceeded that needed for an oil painting of the same size. It took me 3 years to complete over 80 pictures. One of them, entitled *Gongtan Ancient Town*, is 1-meter wide and 4-meter long. Meanwhile, the relocation project of the town has been completed.

In honor of and in respectful memory of the ancient town.

龚滩古镇全景

位于四川盆地东南边陲、渝黔两省交界处，长期以来一直是乌江流域的重镇。明朝万历元年（1573 年），乌江沿岸的凤凰山崩塌，巨石塞江形成险滩，致使航运受阻，货物不得不在此经人力“搬滩”转运，于是各地商贾渐渐云集，古镇成为货物、客商集散中转站，因此而繁荣。1959 年，老龚滩经过三次航道整治，将险滩夷平，此后商贾逐渐散去，经济也逐步衰落。

Panorama of Gongtan Ancient Town

Gongtan, located by the Wujiang River in the southeast Sichuan Basin border, connects Chongqing Municipality and its neighbor Guizhou Province. In 1573, rockslides formed a section of rapids and blocked shipping. The town later became a transfer station where merchants stocked cargo for further distribution. Hence, an ancient town arose.

百步梯

位于古镇的最西端，是进入古镇老街的入口，由青条石铺成，上下落差数十米，甚为陡峭。建成已有数百年，经过岁月的侵袭，条石甚为光滑。

Hundred-Step Ladder

In the extreme west of the town, it is the entrance to an ancient street. The street, paved with green slate, is very steep with a 10-meter drop.

建在小路上的吊脚楼

百步梯尽头建有一座别具特色的吊脚楼，窄窄的石板路从它的下方穿过。从百步梯向下看去，鳞次栉比排列着高低不同的吊脚楼，别有一番韵味。

Stilt Houses on the narrow street

Looking from the hundred-step ladder, there are rows upon rows of stilt houses perched lightly on steep slopes.

阿弥陀佛桥

建于清代。依山势，由条石砌筑而成，桥下有山溪流过，桥一面紧贴路旁建筑。为求平安，人们在路旁墙壁上做了一个神龛，内有阿弥陀佛神像，因此称为“阿弥陀佛桥”。

The Buddha Bridge

Built by the mountain, the bridge was named after the Buddha enshrined in the hillside by the road.

阿弥陀佛桥之石像

神龛中的阿弥陀佛石像，雕刻颇为有趣，既没有寺院神像威严庄重，又没有民间雕刻的细腻精致。浑厚的造型、古拙的刀法，反倒使石像多了一些质朴与亲切的感觉。古镇中并无大的寺院，多种信仰融合在一起，也就形成了独特的雕刻和造型风格。

Statue of the Buddha Bridge

The simple, kind style of the Buddha statue is fully exhibited by its simple design and unsophisticated carving.

杨家客栈

位于新华街，距百步梯250米。原建于清雍正五年（1727年），屡烧屡建，现存建筑由杨芝田建于清宣统元年（1909年）。主楼面街二层，面江三层，南侧依山势而下错一层。它是新华街中最宏大的一组建筑。杨家于明末清初迁徙而来，民国以后杨姓人家或迁走或没落，现已不是杨姓后人居住。

Yang Family Hostel

Yang Family Hostel, located at Xinhua Street, 250 meters from Hundred-Step Ladder, is the street's most splendid group of buildings.

杨家行

昔日龚滩商业繁荣的标志和盛衰的见证。清末民初，杨家成立了"大业盐号"，俗称"老盐局"。大量从四川购进食盐，销售到南方各地。后为官僚资本所控制，生意进一步扩大，就连宋子文也拥有其股份，杨家行名噪一时。其建筑雄踞于二河坝码头附近十余米高台上，俯视乌江，两侧高出屋檐的封火墙，飞檐黛瓦饰以白色墙面，是具有徽州民居和巴渝山地建筑特色的建筑。

Yang Family Merchant Buildings

In the late Qing Dynasty, early Republic China (1900-1920s), the Yang Family established the Great Merchant of Salt, commonly referred as the Old Salt Bureau. Built on the hillside near the Heba Dam Dock, it combined features of Huizhou folk houses and hilly Chongqing.

太平缸

位于老盐局前。老盐局建筑前方为一方形坝子，在寸土寸金的山区显得十分气派，这也正是老盐局选在此处的原因。建筑正对面为一影壁，壁前有一半圆形太平缸（消防水池），缸的外壁嵌有“洋洋得所”。

Peaceful Pot

Peaceful Pot, a large, semicircular pot in front of the Yang Family Merchant Buildings, is used to store water for extinguishing fires.

杨家行的南面

所处地势较为平坦，南北走向、背山面水。从南面看杨家行是山地式吊脚楼，开放性的临江一面带有“耍子”的木结构吊脚楼属于典型的巴地本土风格。整个建筑采用的是传统的穿斗式木结构，具有古镇民居结构的共性。

South of Yang Family Merchant Buildings

The stilt house of the Yang Family Merchant is the traditional wooden column and tie construction, with the usual characteristics of folk houses in all ancient towns.

杨家行前的小巷

龚滩古镇依山而建，镇中小路起起伏伏，连接着高低不同的各个坝子。老盐局前的那段小巷就是连接上下两个坝子的。由于地方狭小所致，老盐局的一部分不得不建在人工搭建的台子上。那段小小的阶梯便被包在了两栋建筑之间了。

Alley before the Yang Family Merchant Buildings

Connecting the upper and lower dam, the narrow steps of the alley in front of the Yang Family Merchant Buildings squeezes between buildings on both sides.

田氏阁楼

依山而建，是古镇中保存较好、较有特色的建筑之一。因地势关系将临路的一面垫起，并未像其他建筑那样用木制柱子支撑，而是有石头筑起坚固的高台，阁楼的一部分建筑便是在高台之上。阁楼为二层前方有一个伸出的廊子，廊子接着长长的石梯通向老街。坐在阁楼之上俯瞰乌江湍流的河水、老街熙攘的人群，自有一番惬意。

Tian Family Loft

Built beside the mountain, the Tian Family loft is one of the well-preserved ancient buildings with unique features. From the loft, the rolling Wujiang River and bustling street crowds can be seen.

田氏阁楼的小院

之所以称它为小院而不是天井，是因为它是利用阁楼和山体之间的一小片空地而形成的，不过是放置楼梯的地方，其宽不过一二米，长不过四五米。有些像苏州园林中的小天井，但与之不同，因其一面为山视野开阔，且为自然天成的景色，别有一番韵味。

Tian Family Loft Yard

This yard,an open area between the loft and the hillside, gives a naturally formed wide view.

2007

田氏阁楼的南面

原先阁楼南面有一些房子，因年久不断损毁，现在为一片山坡。从这里看石台显得格外高大，石台、阁楼、山坡三者的关系看的也越发明显。

South of the Tian Family Loft

Originally, there were some houses south of the Tian Family loft. The houses on the hillside were ruined.

崖边小路

这条小路连接了杨家行和田氏阁楼，最窄处仅有两米宽。一面是靠山的建筑，一面是数丈的悬崖，路上仅有极为低矮的路牙子。第一次在上面走确实有些心虚，但古镇的居民却早已习惯了这种“险境”。

Path by the Cliff

The path by the cliff, connecting the Yang Family Merchant and the Tian Family Loft, is 2-meter wide at the narrowest place.

转角店

位于兴华街中段，因在小巷转角处而得名。原为罗家人所建，因此又称罗家店，旧时曾为盐仓、商号，现为民居。它合理利用地形，与街道有机结合，形成紧凑的布局，同时采用筑台与吊脚相结合的手法，是传统的穿斗式结构建筑。

Store at the Corner

The store, in the middle of Xinhua Street, got its name from its location at the corner. Formerly a salt warehouse, it is now a residence.

半边仓

位于兴华街中段，有 100 多年历史，是古镇重要的仓库之一，见证了古镇的繁荣。作为仓库建筑，其平面简单规整，有宽敞的大门和方便拆卸的横向木板，同时采用筑台方式建造。

Banbian Warehouse (Warehouse with Half Eaves)

100-year-old Banbian Warehouse, located in mid-Xinhua Street, is one of the crucial warehouses of this ancient town.

吊脚楼前

斑驳的青石板铺就的路面没有现代化的气息，它和古朴而优雅的吊脚楼浑然天成，拼出了古镇的文化底蕴。与空地连接的石板台阶从未知的远方延伸至此，显得自然而从容。像这样的石板台阶在古镇随处可见，它将这里的吊脚楼、大木屋、阁楼……甚至是外面的现代文明紧紧地联在了一起。

Front of the Stilt House

Slate steps are anywhere in the town. They connect the stilt houses, the big wooden houses, the lofts with the modern civilization and culture of the world outside.

街景（一）

小镇故事多，但大都发生在这样一个屋檐相对、小楼相依的狭窄街巷里。脚踏青石板，头顶一线天，走上石板街，仿佛走进了一个陌生而亲切的空间，将现代生活的喧嚣与烦躁彻底丢弃，留下的只有属于古镇的天光和云影。

StreetView (1)

Many legends happened in the town, mostly in the narrow streets with stilt houses leaning on each other and doors facing to each other.

街景（二）

石板长街两旁的古民居依地势而建，错落有致，显得庄重得体，毫无夸张炫耀之感。屋檐下的老人在清风逗留的长街中独自洗着衣服。这样一个被岁月定格的画面，不仅体现了当地居民悠闲而平静的生活场景，更是整个古镇的生活态度。

Street View (2)

In the street,breeze lingering, an old man washes alone under the roof – a common scene.

街景（三）

长长的古老的石板街，回响着嘈杂的脚步声。这里一年年一代代被赤脚、草鞋、布鞋、胶鞋、皮鞋踏磨得光滑玉润。青石板街可坐、可行、可卧而无需担忧一身尘土。走在这绝无车踪喧哗的石板路上，一种悠远古朴的历史回归感和传统文化的浸润感油然而生。

Street View (3)

Streets have been ground jade-smooth by bare feet, straw sandals, and cloth, rubber and leather shoes through years and years of generations. People may sit, walk and even lie on it without getting dusty.

郑家岩

位于离郑家自然村千米处的峡谷中。巨大的岩石，酷似狮子头，而狮头上右侧还矗立着一块拔地而起的巨大岩石，俗称印星岩。

Zheng Family Rock

This giant rock like a lions' head, with another huge rock standing erectly on the right, is commonly referred to as Yinxing Rock.

郑家岩旁的吊脚楼

依山就势，静静的矗立在古镇的一角。两层建筑，古朴凝重中透着原汁原味的巴渝风韵，静谧而安宁。这不仅体现了风水理论，更是顺应了自然的特点。

Stilt House by Zheng Family Rock

Built by the cliff, the Zheng family two-storey stilt house exhibits the fine, original taste and style of Chongqing architectures.

大梯子

青石板的阶梯层层而上，一头连着码头文化，一头连着古镇。整个儿大阶梯有成千上百条青石铺就而成，下端是二河坝码头，这里是通向古镇的主要通道。如今，站在阶梯之上，当时商贾云集的热闹景象仿佛就在眼前。

The Long Ladder

The steps of green slates rise up like a long ladder connecting dock and town.

子南茶座

说到“子南茶座”，就不得不提罗子南。他曾是龚滩古镇的一位满腹文史诗书的饱学之士，对龚滩及酉阳的文史掌故了然于胸。这里就是罗子南用抑扬顿挫的重庆方言讲述龚滩传奇的主阵地。如今，这里已经没有当年的热闹，但静静悬挂着的“子南茶座”牌匾，一直是当地居民抓住有关“插座”记忆的那根线。

Zinan Tea House

The tea house is where Luo Zinan, a learned scholar, used to tell legends of Ancient Gongtan.

客栈

吊脚楼式的客栈在龚滩古镇的老街两旁随处可见，它们也是古镇特性的一个体现，成为古镇“身心和灵魂栖居之地”的象征。

Hostel

Stilt house hostels, a feature of Gongtan,are anywhere along the sides of the old streets.

农家小店

一张方桌，四张板凳就可以成就古镇生活的温馨。多年来，不变的是小店门前悬挂着的“古镇土家风味”，而改变着的是一张张来古镇旅游猎奇的新面孔。

Farmyard

A square desk and four benches make for a cozy life in the town.

茶
风
味

通向新街的石梯

典型的山城之路，由不规则的石板铺就而成，仅仅为了方便生活出走而建。这条石梯是通向古镇新街最为方便的道路，远方的新街有着具有古镇特色的客栈，而在那里才是来古镇的第一站，当然这只是对来古镇的游客而言。

Stone Steps to the New Streets

The stone steps, made of irregular-shaped slate, are the typical material of the mountain town.

大屋

石板路从大屋前顺势而下，装点着龚滩人淳朴、粗犷、豪放的风情，用“格子”排列而成的山墙多了几分设计感，其独特的建筑造型之美和浓郁的民俗文化之美被人们称道，它遵循着当地独特的审美规律和文化观念。这种建筑形式真实地记载了当地的人生哲学观和道德审美观，体现了当地的传统文化思想。

Big House

The unique design of the big house amply conveys the special aesthetic and cultural values of local residents.

俯瞰古镇的小路

小路依着山坡顺势向上延伸，几乎呈笔直状，有种通幽的感觉。旁边矗立着的老屋静静的守候于此，增添了几分人文气息。是先有老屋，还是先有小路已不重要。重要的是这里的山、老屋、石阶小路，绘就了一副迷人的人文山水。

Overlooking the path to town

The path stretches up the hillside. The mountain, old house and stepping-stone path are a charming landscape picture of man and nature.

川主庙

位于胜利路，坐东面西，占地面积约 310 多平方米，保存较完整。川主是四川的本土之神，是秦代蜀郡太守李冰的化身，为四川而独有。李冰治水修建都江堰，变水患为水利，造福川民，因此被川人奉为川主。龚滩川主庙始建于清代道光五年（1826 年），已有 180 多年的历史。现川主庙内存有四块石碑，字迹清晰可见。

Chuanzhu Temple

Chuanzhu Temple, at Shengli Road and facing east, was built after 1826 and kept in fine condition. It was the site for offering sacrifices to Chuanzhu, also known as Li Bing. Li Bing, who started building Dujiangyan Dam to regulate the floods and bring benefits for the people, was regarded by Sichuan people as Chuanzhu (Owner of Sichuan).

川主庙戏台

川主庙是祭祀庙宇类型建筑，与其他地方的庙宇布局大体相同，只是受地形限制仅为一进院落。东面为面阔三间的正殿，建筑内部祭祀大堂是穿斗结构，西侧为戏台，全庙建筑格局左右对称。屋脊尾部向上转弯，整个建筑外观看起来活泼轻快。虽然建筑已破败不堪，但仍是古镇居民集会娱乐的场所之一。

Chuanzhu Temple Stage

Chuanzhu Temple is typical architecture of a temple for sacrifice and the main site for rallies and entertainment for town residents.

通向上街的路口

磨得光滑的石板路口，在此可欣赏临江而建、渗透着百年沧桑的古街道、吊脚楼以及那些精美的、抢尽风头的竹编。让人目不暇接，叹为观止。

Gateway to the upper street

From the gateway to the upper street, the stilt houses and the delicate bamboo-woven handcrafts can be fully appreciated.

古镇小巷（一）

和大城市宽大的马路不同，这里的的巷道大都由青石板铺就而成，宽约两米，有种说不出的精致。巷道两边的老房子多是两层，参差的飞檐翘角将巷道上方的天空挤压成一条细细的线。这很容易让人想起吴冠中老先生的国画《老街》，颇有几分相似。

Alley in the Town (1)

The narrow green-slate-paved alley is about 2-meter wide. The skyline over the alley on both sides is a jagged line of flying eaves of the old houses.

古镇小巷（二）

曲径通幽的石板街，转角处会不会有豁然开朗的感觉呢？想要知道答案的话，就去龚滩古镇寻找。也许会有更为让你震惊的景色、场景、或是故事在等待着你去经历、去感悟。

Alley in the Town (2)

The slate-paved alley, winding to secluded places, may suddenly lead to an open area at the corner.

赶集归来的一家人

将幸福打包背在肩上，顺着熟悉的石板街向家的方向走去。一路的嬉笑追打，已经成为这里的风景。这也许就是古镇人独有的纯真和烂漫。

A Family Back from the Fairk

A family walking on the slate street, just returning from the fair, creates a beautiful scene.

编扎手工艺人

竹篾编扎的用品，显示着土家人的手巧心灵。土家花背篓编织精美，可称为竹编一绝。你看，那旁若无人的手工艺人面前多是些形式不一的背篓及生活用品。将自己的劳动成果摆了一地，往往会吸引游人停留。

Weaving Craftsman

The delicacy of Tujia baskets is unique in bamboo handcrafts. All different shapes of baskets and daily supplies attract tourists.

牛角灶

这种灶因其外形弯曲似牛角而得名。古镇上几乎家家户户都有牛角灶。炉上方一般都悬有吊架，是熏制腌腊食品用的。

Ox-Horn-Shaped Stove

Named for its ox-horn shape in each household, the stove with a hanger frame above is used to prepare smoked and preserved food.

织女楼

位于第一关北十余米处，三面皆是绿地，东面邻街，该楼正好处于江边一块突出的小山坡上，左右没有任何建筑，下吊上挑，恰如“空中楼阁”一般。相传150多年以前，一位擅长纺织的姑娘在这座吊脚楼中辛勤的劳作，她织出的布匹、锦缎品相极好，千金难求，因此该楼得名“织女楼”。原来的织女楼已毁，后来在原织女楼的位置建起一座石印社，仍称织女楼。

Zhinü Stilt House

At the north of First Pass on the projecting hillside by the river, Zhinü Stilt House is like a castle in the air. According to a folk legend, the house is named for well-known Zhinü who lived there 150 years ago.

通向山脚的小路

小路以阶梯的形式径直而去，伸向一个类似于北方“天井”的出口。那里有着无尽的天空、优美的景致。好像正在迎接一位不期而来的客人。

Path to the Foot of the Mountain

The path stretches to the foot of the mountain, casually welcoming all guests.

沿江的吊角楼

由远古巢居演变而来的吊脚楼作为一种居住形式，曾遍布西南地区的山山水水，如今已逐渐从我们的视野中消失，所幸地是龚滩古镇还保留了完整的吊脚楼。他们像标本一样在乌江峡谷的峭壁上静静的陈列着，让我们能够一睹干栏建筑的风采。

Stilt Houses along the River

Gongtan, on the cliff along Wujiang Canyon, carefully preserves overhead stilt houses.

吊脚楼下的小路

吊脚楼下面既防潮又通风，同时还不占居生活空间，自然是镇上居民家中最理想的储藏室了。家中的农具、木柴、稻草等杂物全都堆放在此，有的还在此处修葺简易的圈舍，饲养牲畜。临街的吊脚楼下的小路，也让人免受日晒雨淋。

Path under the Stilt Houses

The path under the stilt houses guards people from sunshine and rain and naturally provides storage space for residents.

巨石上的吊脚楼

吊脚楼的正屋一般建在实地上，其余房间除一边靠在实地和正房相连，其余三边皆悬空，靠柱子支撑。吊脚楼有很多好处，高悬地面既通风干燥，又能防毒蛇、野兽，楼板下还可放杂物。吊脚楼还有鲜明的民族特色，被称为巴渝文化的“活化石”。

Stilt House on the Rock

The principal room of a stilt house is normally built on solid ground, while columns support overhead rooms. The stilt house is called the living fossil of Chongqing culture.

拆掉木板的“耍子”

“耍子”是四川话，其基本意思指类似于阳台的建筑部件。吊脚楼的耍子是由从建筑中伸出的木梁和各种木板组成的，拆卸灵活。枯水季时在木梁上搭上木板组成阳台，存放东西；等到汛期乌江水位上涨时，便拆掉木板，减小水流阻力，确保吊脚楼安全。

Balcony of a Stilt House

The stilt house balcony is constructed with protruding beams and planks easily disassembled.

崖边吊脚楼

吊脚楼建在陡峭的山崖之上，有着一副孤傲、倔强的表情。它古香古色，临崖高挑，是龚滩的标志。凿岩垒石，支撑吊脚楼的圆木牢牢地扎根在这些岩石上，历经多年而不动摇，被称为“悬崖上的艺术”。

Stilt House by the Cliff

This stilt house by the cliff is the landmark of Gongtan. It has been standing here intact for years and is entitled "Cliff Art".

夫妻桥

又称为桥重桥，是两座桥重叠成的一座小拱桥。从下面的桥走到上面的桥只需几步石梯。两桥错落有致，弧形优美，气韵流动而不呆滞，桥体并置而不单调，实乃佳偶天成，颇具浪漫情调，因此称为夫妻桥。

Couple Bridge

Couple Bridge is two overlapping arched bridges. The lower bridge is only several steps from the upper one, so it is named Couple Bridge.

崖上人家

望而生畏的山崖总会给人一种距离感，虽然美丽，但只能远观而不能近亵。古镇的山崖往往相反，它会给人一种亲近感，甚至将家安在上面。在此举目环顾，整个古镇尽收眼底，层次分明，有种“一览众山小”的感觉。

Family on the Cliff

Viewed from the cliff, the panorama of the ancient town is perfectly visible to the family on the cliff, bringing a feeling of “viewing all the mountains in a single glance”.

崖上小路

习惯了山崖上的风景，就得习惯通往山崖的小路。这条路几分陡峭、艰险至于也多了几分生活。毕竟路的一头连着大千世界，一头连着温馨的家。

Path on the cliff

Path on the cliff connects the outside world to the cozy home inside.

通向河边的小路

这里没有大海的波涛，也没有江水的激流，有的只是缓缓的河流。看惯了江水的人民，有时也会来到这里感受一下河流的平缓。

Path to the River

Used viewing the rapids, people come here from time to time to feel its tranquility.

邻江人家

滔滔江水已经成为生活的伴奏，习惯了以江水为邻的人家，在外观上看就是多了几分灵气。大大的屋檐，错落有致的房顶，像似在争着捞一把山水的清新。屋檐下晾晒着的衣物，多了几分古镇人家的生活气息，尽管看不到主人的身影。

Riverside Family

Town folk love being the river's neighbor. Clothes hung under the big roof indicate aspects of the riverside family.

吊脚楼和青石板台阶

在青石板台阶面前，吊脚楼一点不显得突兀，楼前反而倒有几分“枯藤老树昏鸦”的感觉。这里，在夕阳西斜，暮色四合的时候，远山近水，包括这古朴斯文的吊脚楼，一下子都变得朦胧起来，渐渐演绎成一幅完美的画卷。

Stilt Houses and Slate Steps

At sunset, stilt houses, slate steps, nearby river and distant mountain are suddenly covered by a veil.

吊脚楼的“耍子”

龚滩的吊脚楼见不到别处的“美人靠”，只是在横梁上挑出一个“耍子”（相当于阳台），就足够谈天说地，消暑纳凉了。邻里之间站在各家的“耍子”上隔空相望、家长里短的聊得不亦乐乎。之间的亲情也都维系在这简陋的“耍子”上了。图中为撤掉底板和围挡的“耍子”。

Balcony of a Stilt House

This is a small, imperfect stilt house balcony,its floor and fence removed.

第一关

位于古镇老街的中部，原为古镇南端的寨门。昔日关北为“城”内，关南为郊外。为防止土匪和歹徒的偷袭，镇民便在这山势险要之地用条石垒砌成了石门。古镇规模不断扩大后，将以前的古镇东大门变成了镇中心。紧挨关门内侧则有一块巨石，在巨石上还留着“第一关”三个大字，据传为明代万历年间李德谷所题。

First Pass

Located in the town center, the First Pass was originally the village south gate. Due to its strategiclocation, past residents converted it into a stone gate to prevent bandit attacks.

夏家院子

夏家祖籍江西，该院子的修建年代不详，估计至少也有 200 年以上历史，现为其后人居住。院子与自然环境巧妙的融合是古镇民居的典型代表。夏家院子位于一个风水极好的地方，它背靠山崖，俯瞰乌江，院旁边的岩石上有千年黄葛树，正门口有宽敞的休息平台。院中的建筑为“一整二横”的凹字型阁楼，临江的一面垒起了不足米高的围墙，整个古镇景色尽收眼底。

Xia Family Courtyard

It is estimated that the Xia Family Courtyard is over 200 years old. A concave building with a low wall under 1 meter, it faces the river. The panorama of the town can be viewed from here. The Xia Family,originally from Jiangxi Province, still live in Gongtan today.

俯瞰乌江

夏家院子“背山面水”，倚凤凰山麓，面朝乌江，又与飞蛾山隔江相对，地处高地无甚阻挡，藏风纳气，被当地居民认为是块“风水宝地”。在夏家正门便可俯瞰乌江，可谓“美景尽收眼底”。

Overlooking the Wujiang River

Xia Family Courtyard is at a perfect place: river in front and mountain behind. The view of the Wujiang seen from its gate is described as “Perfect View All at a Glance”

休息的背妇

山地居民外出来往搬运货物总是背背竹篓。冉家院子门前是一段很陡的阶梯，人们总要在中途休息一下。休息的方式也很特别，从不将竹篓从肩上卸下，而是将一个 T 型木杖垫在竹篓下面来减轻竹篓的重量。也正因如此，人流加之时间的推移，使得这段阶梯上便形成了一个个深浅不一的杵眼。这一个个杵眼见证了古镇昔日繁荣。

A Woman Porter at a Break

Mountain residents use back baskets to carry goods and never take them off when taking a break. Ground down by the back basket sticks, there are marks of different depths worn into the steps.

冉家院子

在古镇，冉家可谓“第一姓”，有“上街不打冉，打冉下不了坎”之说。冉姓又分为高粱冉、疙瘩冉和外来冉。高粱冉是镇中贵族，土司均出自高粱冉。相传冉家院子是冉姓土司修建的花园，至今已有100多年历史，一直由冉姓土司家族居住。现为冉氏后代居住使用。建筑为吊脚楼民居“上宅下店”居住模式，保存较为完整。

Ran Family Courtyard (1)

According to legend, Ran Family Courtyard was built by a family chief more than 100 years ago. It is a well-protected residential stilt house.

冉家院子的大门

冉家院子位于老街中段，处于街道转折变化之处，是老街主要的建筑之一。冉家院子为典型的三合院民居建筑，其平面布局呈梯形，中心有一天井，占地约 150 平方米。它四周封闭，身在其中颇有置身于徽派民居的感觉，但又与徽派民居不同，多了些当地建筑特有的功能性建筑，如活动的门板、二层的廊道等。可谓徽派民居和本地建筑风格融合的经典之作。

Ran Family Courtyard (2)

At the center of the old street, Ran Family Courtyard is one of the town's main buildings. Atypical 3-section courtyard folk building, it combines Huizhou and local architectural features.

绞滩站旁的小巷

龚滩是一段十分险恶的航道，以前需有纤夫将船拉过险滩。20 世纪 50 年代这里建立了绞滩站，用大小型铁质绞盘和钢筋混凝土基盘，配备递缆浮筒、钢缆绳、竹缆绳、棕绳等设施，代替纤夫将船拉过这一险滩。这一时期在长江、乌江沿岸建立起大大小小数十座绞滩站。随着三峡工程的完工，作为中国最后一个绞滩站的龚滩绞滩站也完成了它的历史使命。

Alley next to the Warping Station

The Warping station built in the 1950's was a facility for trackers pulling boats over the rapids.

暖阳

冬季的午后，需要的是一个暖阳，让这里的一切瞬间变得骚动起来。家家都会在暖阳呆着的地方，谈天说地，温馨而幸福。这充分显示了古镇平淡的生活和古镇的安逸。

Warm Sunshine

Chatting in the warm sunshine, cozy and happy,life in the town is leisurely and comfortable.

冉家朝门

南宋建炎三年（1129 年），酉阳寨主冉守忠平定金头和尚起义有功被封为御前兵马使，之后冉氏家族便一直为酉阳之主。元朝改酉阳为宣慰司世袭土司直至雍正年间的改土归流，共传 24 世。数百年来冉氏宗族旁枝蔓延、盘根错节，宗族势力已牢牢掌握了酉阳地区。清末民初，龚滩设分县也是由冉家族人担任县官的，衙署就设在现在的冉家朝门。

作为县衙的冉家朝门基本与周围的民居别无两样，看上去只不过是古镇的大户人家罢了，既无多重的院落有无高大的正堂，也许是山多地少的缘故吧。

Ran Family Court Gate

Youyang Region was under Ran Family's control from 1129 to 1735. Gongtan County was established early in the 20th Century. The Ran Family held county magistrate post and used Court Gate as offices. It was just like other folk houses.

冉家朝门的广场

冉家朝门前有小一广场，设于高台之上，在沿山岩而建的镇上显得颇为气势。原先的小广场上建有县衙大门，现早已无存，但隐约可以看到两边残存的八字墙。也许只有这残存的八字墙默默的见证着当时辉煌。

The Square of Ran Family Court Gate

The square is built on a high platform in front of Ran Family Court Gate. The county institution gate, on this small square, disappeared long ago.

冉家朝门的院子

在古镇的建筑中，冉家朝门的正房算是比较高大、有规矩的，面阔三间，颇有眼压正堂的感觉。正房还有一个独特之处，那就是为了满足县大老爷办公、议事、审案的需要，正方是面向山崖背向乌江，这种设计使它增加了私密性，同时远离了街边的喧嚣。正房与门前的山体围合成的院子在古镇中算是大院子了，院中四周都砌有阶条石，院内条石铺地，还有古老排水系统，这些在古镇的其他院子中都是没有的。

Ran Family Court Gate Yard

The yard enclosed by the principal house and surrounding mountains is the largest in town. It is surrounded by stone steps, paved with block stones, and equipped with an ancient drainage system, not found in other courtyards in town.

小滩子

这是龚滩一处相对平缓的河滩，一些货船常常停靠在这里。沿坡而上有一条长长的传送带就是用来搬运货物的，这条传送带一段连接岸边的船，一边直通老街上的仓库。随着龚滩的慢慢衰落，这条传送带也最终和绞滩站一样退出了历史的舞台。

Small River Beach

This is a relatively flat river beach with a few cargo boats at anchor. There is a long conveyor belt along the slope to carry goods.

董家祠堂

在古镇，董家人口虽不算多，但因世代书香门第，家族中出过不少地方官吏，声望极高。董家祠堂位于老街的中心位置，与川主庙仅一墙之隔，大门与川主庙并列。敢与地方神并肩，并且建有如此规模的祠堂，在龚滩独此一家，可见董家在古镇中的地位和声望。祠堂设在高台之上，需登几十步台阶才能进院。祠堂为一进院，南、北、东三面为二层木楼，有回廊相连；西面为正厅，供奉董氏先人牌位，是家族聚会和祭祀的场所。

Dong Family Ancestral Hall

Located in the center of the old street, its neighbor is Chuanzhu Temple. The Dong Family was not a big family in Gongtan, but it once had quite a few celebrities of good reputation. This ancestral hall is the largest in Gongtan.

通往江边的路

顺着通往江边的石阶望去，仰角 45 度，可见地势的险峻程度。尽管如此，此景在龚滩古镇比比皆是。也许习惯了这种“走险”的生活，才变得平静、无畏。远处的吊脚楼群是一个神秘的土家族苗族聚居之地，是一个能够凝固历史的与世隔绝的秘境。

Road to the Riverside

The steps down to the riverside fall at a 45-degree angle - dangerously steep. But residents here are used to fearlessly walking down the road.

老镇的石板路

斑驳的石板路尽头，拾级而上就到“家”了。对于老屋的主人来说，就该如此。但是作为一名游者来说，这里就是一种温暖。

Ancient Town’s Slate Road

The variegated slate road leads to the home of an elderly owner whose hospitality warms all who come.

小院子

屋檐下干净的路面与上空悬着的屋檐宽度一样，应该是建造时的特殊处理。这样在雨天可以坐在屋檐下聊家常。屋檐下总是会在不经意间发生故事。这里，也许会更精彩。

Small Yard

The road under the roof sheltered by the over-hanging eaves is a special design of the building under which folk enjoy sitting and chatting even on rainy days.

出门的小路

出门就踏上陡峭的石台阶，在山城也不算什么稀罕事，谁叫这里属于山城呢！也就是因为这种在外人看来有点雅致的设计，才造就了龚滩古镇的美丽。

Path Outside the Door

The steep stone steps, right outside the door, help create the beauty of Gongtan.

崖上小院

险要的地势上建造二层楼房，是龚滩古镇的“专利”。长长的走廊、大大的窗户、高高的台阶，大都用木头及竹子建成，着实让人惊叹！

Small Yard on the Cliff

Building two-storey houses in dangerous places is common in Gongtan. The construction materials are mainly stones and bamboo.

倪家院子

位于四方井东的小山坡（凤凰山）上，已建有70年。倪家曾是大户人家，选址在新街东面的小山坡上，地势高，利于防水，历年来从未受到过水灾之苦。倪家院子不靠街，不会受到新街的噪声干扰，较为宁静。图为倪家院子的大门。

Ni Family Courtyard

This building, over 70 years old, is located high up and has never been flooded. Its gate is shown in the sketch.

远眺倪家院子

倪家院子的南面是菜地，其余三面皆是住宅建筑。其利用小山坡的地形与周围建筑形成高低错落的建筑群。倪家院子地势较高、视野广阔。在新街的沿街建筑未建前，可远观乌江、蛮王洞及白水壁。

Overlooking Ni Family Courtyard

The building's high location provides a wide view. The hillside courtyard and the surrounding buildings make a high and low scattered complex.

巨大的黄葛树

别名黄桷树、大叶榕树等，现为重庆的市树。这棵长在山坡上的大黄葛树，少说也有百年以上，是古镇人心中可带来幸福的“吉祥树”了。

Huge Ficus Virens

Growing on the hillside, the huge ficus virens is more than 100 years old and is regarded in the heart of Gongtan folk as the “Lucky Tree”.

古老的纤道

20 世纪 40 年代运盐船只急剧增长，至涪陵的木船已达 200 多艘，至贵州思南的上水船只也有五六十艘，仅拉纤的纤夫、运盐的背夫就达六七千人。纤夫、脚夫们在这条岸边用巨石凿成的纤道上穿流不息，这条古老的纤道见证了龚滩的昔日繁荣景象。

Old Track Road

In the 1940s, the number of trackers making a living along Wujiang River reached 6,000 to 7,000. This old track road witnessed the prosperity of Gongtan Ancient Town.

巨石上雕成的纤道和石梯

龚滩古镇的乌江沿岸，残存着许多在岩石上雕凿成的纤道和石梯。远远看去就像从天而降的瀑布，一泻千里，蔚为壮观。它与雄险崖壁融为一体，形成了“天人合一”的古镇景观。

Track Roads and Stone Steps

Along the Wujiang River in Gongtan, there are many remnants of the track roads and stone steps caved out of the hillside cliffs.

通向中街的石梯

层层叠叠、弯弯绕绕，如通天的云梯，又似巡天的曲廊。顺山势蜿蜒而上，曲曲弯弯，地势起伏跌宕，就像古镇挺起的脊梁，虽略显老态，但依旧活力坚韧。

Stone Ladder to the Central Street

The winding stone ladder, with layers of steps, stretches up into the sky like a ladder of blue cloud or a winding corridor to the sky.

中街上的屋顶

暖阳下的房檐用朴素的砖瓦装饰了百年，在岁月的静静流淌中宛如一副山城画。错落有致的屋顶下藏着的是故事，是生活，是喜怒哀乐…… 在时光的蹉跎中，酿成了一碗老酒，里面多多的是土家人热情。

Roof at the Central Street

The eaves under the warm sunshine,decorated with plain tiles for hundreds of years, look like a mountain painting by gently flowing time.

蛮王洞

处在乌江贵州岸边的万仞悬崖之上，这里不仅藏着乌江流域的神秘，而且也流传着优美动听的故事。洞口的楼阁框架依稀可见，据说这是为“蛮王”塑金身所用。每年正月十五，两岸附近的居民都会到洞里顶礼膜拜。

Cave of the Barbarian King

Located on a cliff with a deep canyon by the Wujiang, the house frame can barely be seen at the cave gate. On the 15th of each lunar new year, residents pay their respects to the Barbarian King.

远望古镇

龚滩古镇的民居依山傍水，用长柱或硬杂木将屋架托起，是为吊脚楼。吊脚楼或凿石为基，或垒石为础，长长的柱头或撑乱石，或绕古树，高低错落。吊脚楼阁长廊迂回曲折，犹如土家民族图腾的各色窗花。

Overlooking the Ancient Town

People here live by the riverside; their houses supported high up on tall hardwood columns are therefore called "stilt houses".

河滩上的山路

看似艰险的路面，有着不一样的经历。对岸河滩上的这块巨石历经岁月的洗礼，慢慢地变成了一条崎岖的山路。

Mountain Road on the River Beach

The huge rocks on the river beach, washed and eroded for years, have been slowly eroded into a rugged mountain road.

荒芜的碎石路

三寸野草，几片碎石装饰着的小路，有着几分寻幽的色彩。碎石路两边杂草丛生，看起来多了几分荒芜，也增了几分惆怅。尽管如此，它依旧是通往对岸码头的道路之一。

Deserted Gravel Road

The small road, adorned with weeds and gravel, leads to a dock on the other side.

对岸的山路

山路是在四面山峰的包围之下开出的一条出行的通路。崎岖的山路，蜿蜒曲折，通向山外的世界。这条历尽沧桑的路上，深深镌刻着几代人的足印，承载着几代人生生不息的朴实梦想。

Mountain Road on the Other Side

This rugged mountain road, stretching to the outside world, is engraved by footsteps and loaded with dreams of many generations.

后　记

本书的画稿从2007年在龚滩古镇实地调研、收集素材归来后开始创作至2009年最终完成，共历时三年。对古镇的眷恋，一直在我心中萦绕，老镇的吊脚楼、老纤道、百步梯、码头、客栈、院子、古桥、古树、古宅也终日是我牵挂。虽然古镇早已整体迁至下游，得到了全面的保护，但古镇那被岁月积淀的一草一木、一砖一瓦却是其他所无法比拟的，因此将套作品整理出版也就成了我多年的一个心愿。

2012年时与我的老师潘守永教授无意聊起了这些画作，可巧的是潘老师长期研究酉阳土家族，对龚滩甚是了解。当他看到这批作品时，也勾起了对古镇深深的眷恋和回忆。在肯定这批画的同时，也积极鼓励我将其整理出版，在他的引荐下有幸结识了学苑出版社的洪文雄老师，同时也完成了我将这批画出版的心愿——将其纳入了《故园画忆》系列丛书中。

在此真诚地感谢学苑出版社的孟白社长和洪文雄老师，有了他们的悉心帮助和指导才有了今天这本《龚滩古镇》。

最后需要说明的是，在我的学习、成长过程中，母亲给予了我巨大的帮助和支持，借此机会向她表示深深的敬意！本书谨献给抚育我成长的母亲——周素琴！